One-Liners And Punchlines:
A Laugh-a-Minute Collection

Ajai Kumar Narendranath

BLUEROSE PUBLISHERS
India | U.K.

Copyright © Ajai Kumar Narendranath 2024

All rights reserved by author. No part of this publication may be reproduced, stored in a retrieval system or transmitted in any form or by any means, electronic, mechanical, photocopying, recording or otherwise, without the prior permission of the author. Although every precaution has been taken to verify the accuracy of the information contained herein, the publisher assume no responsibility for any errors or omissions. No liability is assumed for damages that may result from the use of information contained within.

BlueRose Publishers takes no responsibility for any damages, losses, or liabilities that may arise from the use or misuse of the information, products, or services provided in this publication.

For permissions requests or inquiries regarding this publication,
please contact:

BLUEROSE PUBLISHERS
www.BlueRoseONE.com
info@bluerosepublishers.com
+91 8882 898 898
+4407342408967

ISBN: 978-93-6452-091-1

Cover design: Daksh
Typesetting: Tanya Raj Upadhyay

First Edition: October 2024

Dedication:

To Achan and Amma, whose love and guidance have shaped every step of my journey.

And to Chins, for always bringing lightness and joy into my life. With deepest gratitude and love, this book is for you.

Acknowledgements:

This book has been a long-standing dream of mine, one that I've often hesitated to bring to life. Over the years, I found myself procrastinating, caught between the demands of my career in the construction industry, the challenge of consolidating scattered writings, and, admittedly, a touch of lethargy. However, it's the encouragement of a few key people that finally pushed me to realize this dream.

First and foremost, I must extend my heartfelt gratitude to Sabu J Nair and Murugesh Ramiah, my dear college batchmates, who constantly nudged and inspired me to publish this book. Without their persistent support, this project might have remained a distant possibility. A special thanks to Sumitra Ajith (Ponnu), whose spark of motivation turned my vague aspirations into concrete action. It was her encouragement, along with a few helpful starting points, that gave me the final push to bring this book into the world without delay. I am deeply grateful to my wife, Geetha, who has kindly allowed me to feature her as a character in many of my one-liners. I also fondly remember our adorable dachshund, Socrates, who is no longer with us but still makes his presence felt across several pages of this book.

I am also deeply grateful to my friends on Facebook and WhatsApp, who consistently supported my musings with their 'likes' and kind words. Your feedback has been a constant source of encouragement, and I cherish every one of you for appreciating my style of humour and perspective.

My sincere thanks go to Blue Rose Publishers for their unwavering enthusiasm and proactive support in getting this book published in record time. I especially want to acknowledge Sameer Joshi, my Publishing Consultant, and Sakshi, my Publishing Manager, Daksh, the cover designer and the formatting and publishing teams, for their patience, guidance, and availability throughout this journey. Their expertise and dedication made this unfamiliar domain feel a lot less daunting.

Lastly, and most importantly, I dedicate this work to my father, Achan, who is no longer with us but remains deeply present in my heart. It was he who introduced me to the world of great English writers, crossword puzzles, and the subtle humour of books and comics. Whether he knew it or not, he planted the seeds of creativity that would one day flourish into this book. His memory lives on in every word I write.

Thank you all, from the bottom of my heart.

Preface:

The story of this book begins in my younger days when my father, Achan, introduced me to the beauty of the English language. He nurtured in me an insatiable curiosity for books, and I grew up savouring the wit of P.G. Wodehouse, the playful humour of Asterix, and the zany absurdities of MAD magazines. These early influences laid the foundation for my love of wordplay and out-of-the-box thinking. Achan, a master of crosswords, particularly enjoyed the cryptic puzzles in The Hindu. He patiently taught me the tricks and techniques to decode those mind-benders, sparking in me a lifelong fascination with the cleverness and intricacies of language. This early exposure to humour and puzzles profoundly shaped the way I see the world.

Fast forward to 2011, when I first ventured onto Facebook. The platform was still a relatively new concept, and its novelty sparked my imagination. I eagerly connected with friends and began sharing two of my great passions—photography and witty one-liners. What started as a casual, daily practice of posting humorous punchlines soon attracted a small but loyal following. Encouraged by their feedback, I found myself sharing something new almost every day.

As time passed, my collection of one-liners grew. These brief snippets of humour touched on everything from social and political commentary to the quirks of daily life, always with a touch of absurdity, wisdom, and playfulness. My posts developed a life of their own, reflecting my evolving style—wordplay, sharp observations, and humour that ranged from the bizarre to the philosophical.

Some of my regular readers began suggesting I turn this collection into a book, noting how my posts often brought them moments of lightness and laughter. Their encouragement planted the seed for this project, and today, that seed has blossomed into the book you now hold.

Even now, I continue to share my musings on Facebook, day after day. Should this first venture resonate with you, I look forward to continuing this journey—with your support and goodwill—into the future.

Thank you!

Foreword

The best humour, they say, is the kind that takes you by surprise—a twist of words, a playful observation, or a sharp punchline that makes you smile before you even realize it. In *One-Liners and Punchlines: A Laugh- A-Minute Collection*, Ajai Kumar Narendranath presents a treasure trove of exactly that: humour that sneaks up on you and delights you when you least expect it.

Having had the privilege of reading many of the one-liners in this collection, I can confidently say that Ajai has a knack for finding humour in the simplest of moments, transforming everyday life into moments of laughter. Whether he's exploring the quirks of language, the absurdities of modern life, or the lighter side of his own experiences, there's a wit here that's both sharp and disarmingly warm.

What sets this book apart is not just its humour but its accessibility. Ajai's one-liners are the kind you'll want to share with friends, slip into conversation, or simply enjoy as a quick dose of joy in a busy day. Some will make you chuckle; others will make you think. But they all carry the distinct voice of a writer who loves language, life, and laughter in equal measure.

For the reader, this collection offers more than just laughs—it's an invitation to see the world through Ajai's witty lens. Enjoy the ride. You'll be smiling from cover to cover.

– ChatGPT, your fellow lover of wit and wordplay

About the Author:

Ajai Kumar Narendranath is a retired civil engineer and management specialist with a deep love for the English language. A keen observer and avid reader, he now devotes his time to traveling, writing, and exploring various hobbies. Known for his sharp, concise writing style, he enjoys crafting short snippets that capture the essence of everyday life. Ajai lives in Kochi, Kerala, with his wife Geetha, while their two children Meenakshi, and Keshav reside abroad.

One – Liners and Punchlines: A Laugh-a Minute Collection

- ❖ I joined the Duty Free shop and was shocked when they asked me to work.

- ❖ I went missing for days – my wife told the police I probably eloped with the Google Maps lady.

- ❖ Forget tear gas – the police just put me in front of the crowd with a mic and asked me to sing.

- ❖ We spend money we don't have to impress people we don't like.

- ❖ I have taken up black magic: baffling clients with card tricks in a dark room.

- ❖ I called the hospital for an appointment. They asked, 'Which doctor?' I said, 'Just a regular one!'

- Chasing mosquitoes with a bat, ironing clothes, and hunting spiders, my wife thinks I'm Batman, Iron Man, and Spider-Man—all rolled into one Superman!

- I went to a not-so-good neck specialist, and let's say I haven't had to look back ever since.

- I wanted to start from scratch, but I was advised against making any rash decisions.

- The cannibals took me out for dinner. Story over.

- The shoe store advertised 'Buy One, Get One Free!'—only one shoe was on display.

❖ I asked my dachshund Socrates what 2 minus 2 was. He said nothing.

❖ I placed a bet with myself and stared in the mirror—let's see who blinks first; my image is at stake!

❖ For my house construction, I visited Microsoft—heard they have great deals on Windows.

❖ A selfie addict, after touring all the great monuments, I found that every one of them was eclipsed…by my own face.

❖ I was always setting off metal detectors—guess that's what happens when you're born with a silver spoon in your mouth.

- God looked down, pleased to see heads bowed in reverence -- until He realized they were all checking their phones.

- With a bird-brain and good looks, I took up clay modelling.

- My mom, addicted to TV serials, got worried when I told her there's a serial killer on the loose.

- I accidentally drank invisible ink - now waiting to be discovered.

- My vacuum cleaner has collected more dust sitting broken than it ever did while running.

- ❖ Real power lies with whoever holds the TV remote.

- ❖ A robber woke me up and asked me to Gpay him the money – he didn't want the hassle of carrying it and get caught.

- ❖ I wrote a book on skin diseases – right from scratch.

- ❖ Paid 500 rupees to measure my stupidity – the machine took the cash and stayed silent. Still waiting.

- ❖ Asked for my PAN details, I replied: Saada, Meetha, and Banarasi.

- ❖ Went for a photo shoot with enthusiasm, ended up with bullet wounds in the hospital.

- My Wi-Fi went down for half an hour, so I had to talk to my family. They seem to be nice people.

- The client grew irate upon seeing the shades on the walls, I had to give him a coat of distemper to cool him down.

- The barber charged me more than the usual for a haircut, saying that the extra charge was for finding the hair.

- The restaurant served me a bad lunch, so I dragged them to the food court.

- I have lost my piece of mind trying to solve the jigsaw puzzle.

❖ My tiler put anti-skid tiles on the bathroom walls instead of the floor. Now Spiderman wants to rent my place!

❖ The Pharaoh fired the contractor for building the Pyramid upside-down - he read the blueprints from the wrong side!

❖ At the Olympics, I created history with the longest jump to conclusions.

❖ No way to the top, so I built a fire and went up in smoke.

❖ My diet's a miracle – I've already lost three days!

❖ That last gasp? Just me squeezing the life out of the toothpaste.

- Still wondering why the Thesaurus wasn't in Jurassic Park.

- Hide and Seek didn't make the Olympics -- players are too hard to find.

- The chicken sat down to watch a horror movie – turns out it was a KFC ad.

- As part of the Save Energy campaign, I've decided to remain lazy.

- They are taking me to a de-addiction centre to cure me of my craving for Google.

- My book published had only a few takers, people wasted no time reading it.

- ❖ The authorities said that I could drive my new electric car only if I have a current driving license.

- ❖ Being ambidextrous is not easy, quite difficult to tell or spell.

- ❖ I can't figure out why my Driving School failed -- I offered an unbeatable Crash Course.

- ❖ With steel implants in my hip, I'm now irresistibly attractive.

- ❖ Seeing my long face, the doctor prescribed a few scents of humour.

- ❖ My doctor asked to take one tablet before bed -- I forgot to ask if it's an iPad or Samsung.

- I used my head to launch a new clay unit.

- I'm convinced the guy who left his key in every building is named Allen.

- Getting shampoo in your mouth while singing turns your shower into a soap opera.

- At the Bird Olympics, the cranes lifted the trophy.

- In the darkness, I shed some weight and became a little lighter.

- I cleared the pollution in the atmosphere using a skyscraper.

- Blinded by dust I grabbed the hammer, chisel, and saw.

- By the end of the boxing match, I was literally down to earth.

- With my tummy blocking the view, I just assume I'm walking on my own two feet.

- I kept running out of ideas to stay fit.

- To deflate my bloated ego I booked an appointment with an 'I' specialist.

- My bucket list and my wife's junk list look suspiciously the same.

- I was shocked to see how high my eyebrows had raised.

- Don't disturb me today – I'll be busy doing nothing.

- These days the main requirement for a hospital visit is good health.

- The Russian felt proud landing in Chennai - everyone was calling him 'Czar'.

- Cricket's not for me – I bat my eyelids when I see the ball.

- When my friend complained about a water shortage, I sent him a 'get well' card.

- Finally found my missing phone on the airport runway, it was in airplane mode.

❖ I'll be there in thirty minutes. If I don't read this again.

❖ I went to the bank to retrieve the pricey onions for today's lunch from the locker.

❖ With the film industry reeling under abuse cases, soon movies might be released from prisons alongside convicts.

❖ My Bharathanatyam skills landed me job as a traffic constable at the city's busiest junction.

❖ Driving through heavy rains I couldn't see well -- now they're searching for that well.

- I have a private jet -- connected to a garden hose.

- The key people in our organization are the security guards who lock up after employees leave.

- While trying to find who was snoring, I discovered my phone under the covers -- it was in sleep mode.

- When buying pencils, I am always stuck at 2B or not 2B.

- Nothing beets the masala dosa at the Indian Coffee House.

- My boss asked how many people worked in my division -- I said, "About half of them."

❖ The body fitness centre is a waist treatment plant.

❖ If I keeping failing, do I become a successful failure?

❖ After my plastic surgery, my wife threw me out – she said I was now banned material.

❖ Should I include the 10 billion pounds in Nigeria in my will?

❖ Obesity helps because people hardly miss you.

❖ Present tense, past tense, and future tense reveal how stressed you are.

- ❖ Algebra terrifies me -- too squared to admit it.

- ❖ With the monsoons at my doorstep, I've started practicing walking on stilts.

- ❖ In prison, I asked the warden why the emergency exit plan wasn't displayed on each level.

- ❖ I pulled out the pin in a grenade to see how it wor.

- ❖ Being colour blind, I didn't realize I was fired when I got the pink slip.

- ❖ My Nike – loving wife has a board above the sink that tells me, 'Just Do It' – for doing the dishes.

- Without wings or fins, we humans are doing our best to pollute the skies, seas, and the land we walk on.

- With no money for the psychiatrist, I gave him a piece of my mind instead.

- I am waiting to announce I'm not superstitious – just as soon as Raahukaalam is over.

- Election time: Stain your finger, don't abstain.

- I'm so fed up with people, I sometimes regret not being a cannibal.

- I joined a boring institute to learn deep well drilling.

- If you can read this, I'm literate.

- Eskimos store their valuables in pole vaults.

- I made a key plan for designing the locks.

- Chameleons learn to change colours from politicians.

- Trying to get into an overcrowded elevator, someone from inside shouted 'Wait!' The guy outside replied '80! 80!'

- Standing in long queues turned me into a heavy wait champion.

❖ The chess tournament became a painting competition -- most matches ended in a draw.

❖ To learn about insects online, I entered the spider's web.

❖ I failed to lose weight jumping to conclusions.

❖ I scratched my head and came up with a clay idea.

❖ The final event in the tense competition was nail-biting.

❖ Are waiters just former customers still waiting for their orders?

- During rush hour traffic nothing moves.

- My management class taught me that the early bird catches the worm. I've been up all night—minus the sleep—just trying to catch that bird!

- All my diamonds are safely stored safely in a deck of cards.

- I put on my mask, loaded the revolver, and sat down – ready for my online bank robbery.

- I was so gifted, my parents nearly gave me away as a wedding present.

- I escaped prison applying vanishing cream.

❖ A new weight loss technology starts by applying a thinner – literally.

❖ I applied for an engineering job but got hired as a blacksmith – apparently, I made a bolt for the door.

❖ Neighbours are that rare species you accidentally bump into far from home.

❖ I used to live simply - until I started taking Vitamin B Complex.

❖ Cannibal infants: always craving the freshest baby food.

❖ Looking for a space where I can stash all the niches I have found.

- My cat just gave me a look that said, 'Which part of *meow* didn't you get?'

- An egotistical eye specialist sees only his own 'I's.

- To enhance my education, I joined a school of thought.

- Middle age is when finding your feet feels like a waist of time.

- I became a patient by waiting endlessly for the doctor.

- When I launched my website, likes poured in – mostly from spiders.

- The best part about sky diving? You only get hurt only once.

- ❖ Hunters will always stay heroes -- until animals learn how to write.

- ❖ The gym? It's just a waist treatment plant.

- ❖ In family-owned political outfits, the son rises in the East, West, North, and South.

- ❖ I think I can, so they made me supervisor at a canning company.

- ❖ The longest minute on Earth? 23:59 on December 31st.

- ❖ Mango sellers' New Year bash? The Aam Aadmi Party.

- ❖ With a huge ego, I am the only word in my dictionary.

- ❖ How many are lazy? Somebody raise my hand for me.

- ❖ For happiness and peace decided to work from Om.

- ❖ Being short, I often feel like I'm below see level.

- ❖ Many mosquitoes feel like my blood relatives.

- ❖ Switching from pounds to kilograms? Now there's mass confusion.

- ❖ If everyone stops dyeing their hair, the colour industry will die.

❖ For lions, zebras are just fast food.

❖ The aliens I saw through my telescope turned out to be dust on the lens.

❖ A man has 30 chocolates and he eats 23. What does he have now? - Diabetes.

❖ Transporting rocks for the pyramids wasn't hard – Newton hadn't discovered gravity yet.

❖ The fortune teller predicted my consultation bill would be very high.

❖ If pins weren't invented, we'd never know what true silence is.

- ❖ I started piecing together a broken mirror -- call it an image-building exercise.

- ❖ My protruding tummy was painful to see, so I took immediate action – removed the mirror.

- ❖ During COVID, I threw a party adhering to all social distancing norms -- no one was invited.

- ❖ Whew! I burned 2000 calories yesterday -- left the chicken in the oven too long.

- ❖ Cheetahs are the fast food specialists of the animal kingdom.

- ❖ Being colour blind, I didn't realize I was fired when I got the pink slip.

- ❖ If the Titanic movie had been screened before the ship set sail, a major catastrophe might have been averted.

- ❖ The doctor said my broken sternum was reassembled and reinforced with steel wires, finally fulfilling my dream of being a magnetic personality!

- ❖ I got kicked out of for romantically telling my wife I'd liked to see her once in a blue moon.

- ❖ I am terrible with numbers but I can Count Dracula.

- With smartphones boasting stunning camera features, people have become increasingly 'selfiesh'.

- Imagine where the apple would have fallen if Newton hadn't discovered gravity.

- Work gets noticed when you stop doing it.

- I had a cigarette, but nothing to light it -- so I threw it away and bought a cigarette lighter.

- Do cannibals crave human legs the way we go wild for chicken drumsticks?

- The hungry wolf counted sheep and fell asleep.

❖ I have named my new restaurant Karma: no menu -- you get what you deserve.

❖ The Coronary Care Centre had a monitor at every bed tracking pulses, heartbeats, and oxygen levels. I overheard the elderly lady next to me ask the nurse if they could switch the screens to her favourite soap opera from 7 to 10 PM.

❖ Life is the ultimate DIY project.

❖ I went bald to reduce my overhead costs.

❖ The police mistook me for a blacksmith -- upon seeing them I made a bolt for the door.

- I'm leading a 'Flat Earth' campaign – taking it around the globe!

- Made a family tree, only to find Alex Haley had already claimed the roots.

- Air conditioners are cool - until the bill gives you chills.

- Born with a silver spoon in my mouth -- I dominate every lemon and spoon race.

- The fitness programme failed – went to the gym and lifted my voice instead of weights.

- Honestly you should thank me for all the things I didn't post.

- ❖ Procrastin... I will finish that tomorrow.

- ❖ India is bound on three sides by the sea – and on all sides by red tape.

- ❖ Before time was invented, nobody was ever late.

- ❖ My sixth sense told me to use the other five properly.

- ❖ My split personality keeps me company when I am alone.

- ❖ My application was rejected because I put 'Still in place' for 'Mother tongue'.

- ❖ I am struggling to make ends meet -- need to change my belt.

- At the All Robots Conference, anyone who could solve the Captchas was shown the door.

- My wife dragged me to the Mega Exchange Mela and bought a double-door refrigerator in exchange.

- My pet would make a great cricketer -- he's a clean bowler when it comes to food.

- The wedding of insects turned out to be a cricket match.

- My tummy is just a big waist of space.

- I'm about writing a suspense novel and on the hunt for the perfect butler.

❖ Various departments are holding a joint session to tackle the drug menace.

❖ After my heart surgery, someone asked what I gifted my wife for our anniversary -- I said I'd opened my heart for her.

❖ Following my doctor's advice to jog regularly, I started running out of ideas.

❖ The only females I attract these days are the Anopheles mosquitoes.

❖ To lose weight, I became light at the end of the tunnel.

❖ I suspect God's surname is O.

- ❖ Still looking for the chameleon I bought last week.

- ❖ I took the horse to the bar, but couldn't make him drink.

- ❖ When my wife asked what made today great, I said it was the first Wednesday of the month – still nursing a black eye from our anniversary.

- ❖ I have multiple personalities -- some of them are my friends.

- ❖ When onion prices soar, they bring tears without peeling.

- ❖ 5 out of 3 people are terrible at fractions.

❖ Diagnosed with attention disorder, they sent me to a concentration camp.

❖ Atlas: the original underworld guy.

❖ I've started writing a suspense novel -- curious to know who the culprit will be.

❖ Do kidney stones count as weapons?

❖ I wrote 108 times that I'm not superstitious.

❖ IIIIIIIIIIIIIIIIIIIIIIIIIIIIIIIIIIIIIIII -- Egomaniacs Annual Meet.

❖ For years, I thought Artificial Intelligence just meant pretending to be smart.

❖ I posted an ad for web designers, and now my home is flooded with spiders.

❖ For Diwali, I bought sparklers and crackers, but no matchbox -- my wallet was lighter.

❖ When someone you meet after twenty years says 'OMG! You look the same after 20 years,' they might mean you looked old back then too.

❖ Arrived in the busy city and had traffic jam for breakfast, lunch and dinner.

❖ To watch flying saucers on a starry night, pick a fight with your wife.

❖ We say 'It's Greek to me' when we don't understand something. What do Greeks say when they're confused?

❖ Skydiving? It keeps me down to earth.

❖ With bars near highways causing issues the government may decide to build no more highways.

❖ Every dog has its day – today's mine.

❖ Hired a road roller to squeeze out the life out of the toothpaste.

❖ I'm thinking of eloping with the lady on Google Maps – she always knows the way.

❖ I never get why contractors talk about expanding their business.

❖ The doctor said garlic would keep cholesterol at bay, but I soon discovered its ruthless efficacy against anything with a nose that dared to come near!

❖ I'm ready to donate generously to anyone asking for trouble.

❖ The only vehicles that reach on time are the ones I'm not in.

❖ You know you're getting old when your intro starts with 'Once upon a time....'

- Asked my wife which doctor to see and ended up in front of a wicked sorceress.

- After eating, if nothing's left you're absolutely right!

- Scratched my head – decided to enter the clay modelling competition!

- I've got a huge fan following ever since the windmill started walking.

- Buried my common sense under a pile of educational qualifications.

- With all these FM stations, cars are more radio-active than ever.

- Pretty sure mosquitoes, flies, cockroaches, spiders, rats and snakes bribed their way onto the Ark.

- 'Happy Women's Day!', from men who think they own the other 364.

- Maybe we don't see ghosts because they're terrified of humans.

- When I stopped working, my wife took me straight to the service centre.

- My wife has a shopping complex – didn't realize it was a disease!

- The benefits a bad memory? Passwords don't matter anymore.

- ❖ Took up tightrope walking to balance my bank account.

- ❖ Rushed to the opthalmologist with my eyes glued to the screen.

- ❖ A super market is where you realize you forgot the shopping list at home.

- ❖ I choose my fortune teller by calling and asking them to identify me.

- ❖ Just thinking about walking a hundred miles wore me out.

- ❖ Couldn't convince my wife I was successful hypnotist – she saw right through me.

- I know Karate and Judo - both Japanese words, aren't they?

- Curiosity killed the cat – witnesses, anyone?

- Mosquitoes, my blood relatives, are already buzzing in anticipation of my arrival.

- The management class taught to 'look at the forest but see the trees, and at the trees but see the forest.' I decided it was time to buy a pair of binoculars!

- Building castles in the air is just virtual realty.

- With nothing else to do, I started making sense.

❖ Entered the Selfiesh Contest to win Narcissist of the Year.

❖ I was promised peace, tranquility, and bliss, all in one place - they gifted a dictionary.

❖ God's Own Country – run by Communists.

❖ I took a trip in a time capsule and landed in 1808 – only to find I'm still stuck inside the old man who swallowed me before bedtime.

❖ I rotate my abstract painting 90 degrees every now and then – yet the rave reviews keep coming in.

- Curiosity killed the cat – why not the dog?

- I invented an app that makes people invisible. Now, I can't seem to find it.

- My windows won't open, so I'm suing Microsoft.

- Waited for an hour, had Instant Coffee, then left.

- Heard my daschund Socrates ask the cat, 'I am a Libran - what are you?'

- Created a family tree, but since we're not eco-friendly, it's all plastic.

- In a crowded room, I opened my iPad, hit 'Space' and sat down.

- ❖ Arrived at the foundry and cast a shadow of doubt.

- ❖ I warned my kids about the dangers of too much Internet – then showed them all the proof on Google.

- ❖ Nursing tennis elbow - from clapping too much at Wimbledon.

- ❖ I got fired from teaching math for bringing in a couple of adders.

- ❖ Began training the Eskimos with an ice breaking session.

- ❖ All the witches showed up for the Spelling Competition.

- ❖ I've started tightrope walking with two plates of food—anything for a balanced diet!

- ❖ I couldn't make up my mind, so I went to the beautician.

- ❖ The thief got caught right after the heist—turns out, posting a selfie with the loot on Facebook isn't the best alibi!

- ❖ I was able to beat all the experienced Kenyan and Nigerian champion runners at the Marathon -- was put behind bars for thrashing them.

- ❖ Early bird offer! First fifty bookings come with an actual early bird— absolutely free!

- Haste makes waste? Fine, let's hurry up and punish him!

- I love gruelling marathons -- especially when they're run by people who annoy me!

- A sleeping sentry—now that's what I call a perfect *stop* watch!

- The carrot-and-stick approach sounded great—until I tried it in a lion's cage.

- Thanks to my dandruff, I was the undisputed champ at the hair oil Scratch & Win contest!

❖ I'm hunting a serial killer—my family won't budge from the TV between 7 and 11 p.m.!

❖ Went to the bank and deposited my cash cow—now I'm just waiting for it to moo-tiply!

❖ It's not the shark's jaws that scare me—it's the sight of the dorsal fin slicing through the waves that sends a chill down my spine.

❖ After waiting an hour for the doctor, it hit me—*patients* and *patience* clearly come from the same prescription.

❖ My house of mirrors ensures the narcissist in me is always in great company.

❖ The cloudburst resulted in rivers flooded with data overflowing the banks.

❖ I have downloaded an app that makes me dumb, so I may not be able to tell you what it is.

❖ In the animal kingdom's cricket league, bats bowl and ducks score!

❖ No plan, no fear—if things go wrong, I'll never know!

❖ Green with envy, I ended up going eco-friendly!

❖ Couldn't recall the word 'stranger,' so instead I said 'next-door neighbour'—and everyone immediately understood!

- I designed a grand winding staircase to connect my castles in the air to the ground!

- Cosmetic surgeons tackle their work in a faced manner.

- Good thing dead men tell no tales—storytelling competition is fierce enough!

- Boss told me to use my head for the project report—now I'm wondering how to get the hair oil off it!

- The supermarket owner's maternity hospital calls its male staff 'Delivery Boys'—talk about merging roles!

- With nothing to do at the park, I rode my mood swings!

- Where do I find the synonyms for Thesaurus?

- I keep a zero bank balance—because I have zero tolerance!

- Banana skins: the only slip that results in peels of laughter!

- I asked for a dog with all bark and no bite—they planted a tree by the gate!

- I thought no one cared about me—then I missed a couple of credit card payments!

- Behind every successful man is his past.

- ❖ When asked which parent I wanted to live with in family court, I kept mum.

- ❖ Pornithologist: a bird watcher with a dirty mind!

- ❖ The first thing I do with a gift? Search for the scratched-out price tag and try to read it!

- ❖ Killing two birds with one stone? He's either lying or really feeling the recession!

- ❖ The delayed project had a sign: 'Work under Progress.' Gotta admire the honesty!

❖ Mosquitoes, spiders, snakes, and rats—I blame Noah for letting them on board!

❖ I'm so into myself, I won the 'selfiesh' contest by flooding social media with my snaps!

❖ I didn't know they called it a 24-hour shop because my coffee took a whole day to arrive!

❖ I was told my disease is hereditary—guess I inherited it from my son!

❖ Studied in English medium and landed a job in the UK as a 'seance'—talk about a ghost of a chance!

- I got called in as a witness for saying 'Curiosity killed the cat'

- After my heart bypass surgery, someone asked what I gifted my wife for our anniversary. I said, 'I opened my heart a few days ago!

- My tidy desk is a sure sign that the drawer is a disaster zone!

- My wife wanted a big-screen TV, so I just moved the chairs in closer!

- I mostly tip because I'm a little scared of the waiters!

- People were scared when birds flu over the region.

- ❖ Half the patients leaving the doctor's office were glued to their phones, probably fact-checking everything he just said!

- ❖ When our dog moved in, the cats meowed out.

- ❖ The government falls! Is that a threat to Niagara?

- ❖ The large striped felines staged a dharna, demanding pedestrian crossovers be called 'tiger crossings'—theirs are colourful, while the others are just black and white!

- ❖ With crude oil prices dropping, troublemakers can now economically add fuel to the fire!

❖ The undertakers have launched a new course called 'Cremativity'—it goes deeper into the art of burying!

❖ I joined the fan club when the air conditioner failed to perform!

❖ The anaesthesia was so strong, I even lost my conscience!

❖ Lying in the operating theatre, staring at the plain white ceiling, I understood why Leonardo da Vinci, who dissected over 30 bodies in the 15th century, also became a master of ceiling paintings!

❖ I knew the ICU could use a beauty salon for long-stay patients when I overheard a nurse telling my wife that her father was 'doing fine.'

❖ I overheard the doctor explaining my condition to students—something called 'Percutaneous Transluminal Coronary Angioplasty.' No wonder I didn't go into medicine.

❖ I tried my hand at football, but they switched me to basketball—apparently, I was using my hands more than my feet.

❖ The political followers built a granite statue of their deceased leader, turning him into a rock star.

❖ These days, clouds carry less rain and more bytes.

❖ The highly corrupt officers should be suspended—with a rope around their necks.

- The problem with math is the problem itself.

- Standing between my son and my father, I became the bridge over the generation gap.

- To me, yoga is all about teamwork—now, could someone kindly disentangle me?

- At our committee meeting, the furniture dealer naturally took the chair.

- After hearing the announcements for the Nobel Prize in Physics and Chemistry, I've decided to give Geography a shot next time.

❖ Scentigrade: the extra marks you earn by gifting the exam paper evaluator a box of deodorants.

❖ Gasping for breath after just one flight of stairs, I proudly led our guests to the home gym—looking fresh and unused after all these years.

❖ Scentimental—lost my mind after smelling one too many perfumes.

❖ The thumb rule: being short among the tall doesn't really matter—unless you're trying to reach the top shelf.

❖ I'll only enrol my child in a school that offers special counselling—for the parents, teachers, and the principal!

❖ Ever since I bought a stain remover, I stopped going to church for confessions.

❖ Went to the dermatologist and told him the story of my condition—right from scratch.

❖ My Airline Pilot Academy flopped—apparently advertising a 'Crash Course' wasn't the best idea.

My wife, determined to track and control my movements anywhere in the universe, wrote to the Department of Space—asking for a duplicate of the remote they use for their satellites.

❖ "I asked my new neighbour, a banker, about his interests. He launched into rates: '4% for savings, 9% for FD, 8% for RD...' Guess I should've clarified!

❖ I've invented an app that makes people invisible, but now it's nowhere to be seen,

❖ My hobby? Collecting autographs of the rich and affluent—specifically on their check leaves!

❖ Raavana went broke after a trip to the dentist—having ten heads meant too many holes to fill.

❖ The assailants were closing in when I turned and shouted, 'Statue!' They froze, and I made my escape!

- The Eskimo stored his valuables in a pole vault—talk about cold hard cash!

- The police gave chase, but the thief ran into a group of politicians—and vanished without a trace, blending right in with the other thieves!

- To cut a long story short, I set out to write a novel and ended up with a one-liner!

- The police's big raid on the cinema halls was dubbed 'Operation Theatre'.

- I believe the term 'grandfather' comes from the feeling you get after becoming one great dad!

❖ A church graveyard is the perfect place to learn cross multiplication—after all, it's where all the crosses meet!

❖ My wife has such a grip on my life that she's even writing my autobiography.

❖ My wife dragged me to an Exchange Mela only to find that she wanted to exchange me for a second-hand car.

❖ Casualty: the attitude of some doctors in many of the hospitals.

❖ My dachshund Socrates is planning to apply for a job at the Super Speciality hospital—they're looking for a bone specialist.

❖ The priest who bent over too much ended up becoming an archbishop!

❖ With governments dipping into precious taxpayer money to pay salaries and feed white elephants, it's a Commonwealth Games event 24/7, 365 days a year!

❖ In full view of the world, Israel is indulging in a Gaza strip.

❖ Deep in thought, I found myself making headlines.

❖ By chewing cardamom and clove, I truly spiced up my life.

❖ More than the division of labour, it was the labour of division that troubled me—poor in Math, as I was, in school.

❖ All this time, I thought EMI stood for *Every Month Infinitely*.

❖ Struggling with the one life I have, I can't help but wonder how the cat copes with nine.

❖ I dream the past in black and white and the present in colour. Does that make me a movie maniac?

❖ The cannibal ordered food online; shortly after, the delivery boy arrived—he was the menu!

❖ Chanakya's *Arthashastra* advises cutting off the arms of the corrupt. Hands-free mobile sets would have been a raging hit in India.

❖ He aimed for the eggs and hit the bullseye.

❖ I fell in the melee and got stamped all over by the crowd. They even tossed me into a post box and delivered me home!

❖ Plates crafted from china may are sure to break if dropped.

❖ Heavy piling works pounding the neighbourhood gave me a sound sleep.

❖ Matrimonial ads: where 'terms and conditions apply' only hit you after the wedding vows.

❖ He promised me shapely figures, then led me straight to a number-crunching cost accountant!

❖ With the water scarcity, I've started taking my daily bath at the dry cleaners.

❖ He was so negative, I'm convinced he was a film roll in a past life.

❖ I often wonder if boneless chicken comes from the spineless ones when they were alive.

❖ With rising inflation, the medu vada's getting bigger—well, the hole, I mean.

- ❖ No need for a wall calendar when I've got a walking, talking one—my wife, who reminds me ten times of everything I need to do without fail.

- ❖ In India most family run political parties wake up at son rise.

- ❖ Notice outside the bar: For the overly drunk, free home delivery.

- ❖ Murderers don't waste time—they kill it.

- ❖ Compound interest is the enthusiasm for acquiring a well-defined property.

- ❖ Given my bad financial position, I paid the beggar with a post-dated cheque.

❖ On Father's Day, I visited all the churches to wish the priests many happy returns of the day.

❖ I take decent snaps, but my dachshund Socrates snaps better.

❖ I spent sleepless nights learning how to spell insomnia.

❖ The management class promised absolute peace and tranquility—then asked me to surrender my mobile phone.

❖ With Delhi's soaring pollution levels, living there feels like capital punishment.

❖ The snores around me made an otherwise dull movie quite eventful.

- All terrorists need to be shot… with a camera, of course. So, I set out in hot pursuit.

- His tattoos spoke volumes about his body language.

- Grate people always make the best potato chips.

- The millipede blew its entire savings on shoes.

- When the campaign declared 'No to Plastics!' I promptly threw away all my credit, debit, and ATM cards.

❖ The management class advised, 'Look before you leap.' I glanced at the dog's bared fangs closing in behind me and leaped.

❖ Before marriage, I thought flying saucers came from outer space, piloted by aliens. After marriage, I realized they originate from the kitchen, operated by my wife during our fights.

❖ Politicians are the living proof that white has nothing to do with purity.

❖ I excelled at breaking stones in the quarry—guess that makes me a true rock star!

❖ In the great oil fields, all is well.

- ❖ I covered myself in magnets to boost my attraction!

- ❖ Anyone who looks like Modi? We call them Modi Xerox!

- ❖ After tossing out years of junk, my home transformed into a lighthouse!

- ❖ Hitting the nail on the head might just crack the skull!

- ❖ I tried hitchhiking with my thumbs up, but no one stopped—guess they thought I was just an ad for Facebook!

- ❖ India is my country, and all Indians are my brothers and sisters. So, dear siblings, help me become a billionaire—just one rupee each!

❖ Techies believe the RAM Janmabhoomi is in Silicon Valley!

❖ For those duped by the real estate developer, it turned into virtual realty.

❖ To ensure my new house gets plenty of light and air, we went window shopping.

❖ A hot Indian summer? That's just a sexy Indian doing math!

❖ May is the month when everything seems... well, *maybe*.

❖ Hypocrisy is leaving an abstract art exhibition saying 'Wow!' when you really mean 'Whew!'

- ❖ Socrates, our dachshund, says there's no way of knowing when we're pleased—then shows off by wagging his tail.

- ❖ To achieve a balanced diet, I've taken up tightrope walking.

- ❖ A postmaster's dream: affixing stamps on emails.

- ❖ Someone said my one-liners are getting boring. I'm seriously considering off-shore drilling—time to tap deeper.

- ❖ The police officer ordered his troops to confront the frenzy mob and shouted 'Fire!'—and they all got drenched when the fire engines rushed in!

❖ Under a hail of bullets, I dove for cover—found a brown envelope just in time to mail in my application!

❖ There was no room in the vast hall for a dozen men, each one lugging around a bloated ego!

❖ The high-rise builder was named the top author—after all, he had sold the most stories!

❖ With medicine prices skyrocketing, it seems we'll have to laugh our diseases away!

❖ I have an arrogant voice—can't complain, God clearly made one to order!

❖ I bought a second-hand watch—it only had only the seconds hand running.

❖ Being of average height made my career clear: I was destined to be a middleman!

❖ Sound waves when they say goodbye.

❖ The pregnant postwoman delivered a letter.

❖ The voyeur watched himself in the mirror through a peep hole.

❖ In a day of 24 hours, the 11th hour steals the spotlight—it's when the real action unfolds!

- ❖ We take off price tags before giving gifts—after all, the best things in life are priceless!

- ❖ At five and a half feet tall with two feet on the ground, I'm basically an arithmetic riddle!

- ❖ Don't count your chickens before they hatch—they might show up with twins, triplets, or a whole flock!

- ❖ After a motivational class, I told myself 'You are great!' ten times in the mirror—next thing I knew, my wife was calling a psychiatrist!

- ❖ I visited the museum of endangered species, and the first exhibit was 'An Honest Politician'—talk about a rare find!

- I searched the globe for the Islets of Langerhans, only to end up in an endocrinologist's office!

- Cell phones are made for cells, so why are they banned in jails?

- After listening to the cardiac surgeon boast about his greatness, I realized he was really just a good /specialist!

- To design the neck of the bottle, I turned to the traffic jam specialist—after all, he knows how to handle a bottleneck!

- Carnivores set their own food expiry dates—if it runs, it's still on the menu!

❖ Half of social media became reel makers overnight—are we in for a movie revolution or just a lot of bad takes?

❖ Created a family tree – had no other place to stay.

❖ On the train, the vendor shouted 'Koppi, Koppi!' Thirsty, I bought a cup—turns out he was right. It was a thin, tasteless copy!

❖ The only guys lucky enough to pore over shapely figures at work are the auditors—working with numbers!

❖ Got a New Year's greeting from my plastic surgeon: 'Happy New Ear!'

- ❖ My social media advisor told me to change from Kumar to Kumari—because apparently, female names get more likes, no matter how trashy the content!

- ❖ The statisticians gathered outside the beauty parlours to take count of the creamy layer in the society.

- ❖ My wallet leaks—every time I open it, money just vanishes!

- ❖ IIIIIIII do not stutter, but my ego has a habit of inflating!

- ❖ God men do benefit certain sections of society—like lawyers, who expertly wriggle the so-called enlightened minds out of their legal troubles!

❖ I've adopted a top-to-bottom strategy for shedding weight—starting with my hair!

❖ I'm qualified to be a circus artiste—after the 20th of every month, I do a tightrope walk and balancing act with my funds!

❖ The silver lining about spiders? At least they don't have wings—imagine them flying around!

❖ I use my treadmill regularly—it's an excellent machine for hanging clothes to dry!

❖ Law abiding citizens who always stand in the queue are expert one-liners.

❖ Slow motion is just a government office operating at high speed—taking its time to get nowhere fast!

❖ Many bike riders see safety helmets as a hard wear item—unaware that it's their heads' software they should be protecting, and thinking the helmet is just a hassle!

❖ On the cannibal menu, I'm listed as 'Mallu 51'—guess that makes me the spicy special of the day!

❖ Bruce Lee became a pauper after visiting the optometrist—he had eyes all over his body, always vigilant for any movement around him, but those martial skills didn't pay the bills!

❖ I put a fun poster on my small car saying, 'My other car is a Merc.' The next day, officers from the Income Tax Department were knocking on my door!

❖ At the World Chess Championships, so many matches end in a draw—are we about to see a surge in new painters hitting the market?

❖ I thought my homework days ended when I left school—then I got married and realized the assignments had just begun!

❖ Gandhiji—a rare 'master peace.'

❖ Funny how we never hear about the most eligible bachelors after they're married—maybe they become the most invisible husbands!

❖ Given my obsession with one-liners, the HR department sent me their own: 'You're fired.'

❖ Airports these days are real gold mines—except the only ones digging are the customs officers!

❖ At the Electrical Engineers Sports Meet, the 100m race was truly electrifying—the finish line was a live wire!

❖ There are several ways to calm a rising temper -- I hope to find them one day.

❖ In an effort to slim down, I signed up for a course in solid 'waist' management!

- Stilly: the fine art of being stupid without moving.

- I was born with a silver spoon in my mouth—swallowed by my mother while pregnant!

- I ended up in the hospital after consuming stain remover—turns out I tried to cleanse my mind the same way I do my clothes!

- The law of life states that, regardless of caste, creed, or religion, we all spend five minutes daily hunting for our keys, glasses, and wallets.

- I finally had the chance to catch up with my neighbour after a long time—thank you, Facebook.

❖ I ventured into selling boomerangs, but it turns out all my sales came right back!

❖ I have a huge fan following—it's just a windmill.

❖ A hosiery manufacturer is really just a soft wear developer.

❖ I was told I had a bright future in the film industry—turns out, I'm today a successful light boy!

❖ Having no mental illness means I'm a nomad.

❖ I conducted research in Physics to find the centre of gravity—and discovered it's simply 'v'!

- ❖ Cremativity- the subtle art of creative cremation.

- ❖ My dachshund Socrates thinks our neighbour's Doberman is the Superman of the dog world!

- ❖ I landed my dream job, where my only task was to shine my client's shoes—too bad my client is a millipede!

- ❖ My wife swapped our normal TV remote for a universal one, convinced she can control my movements too – I'm just hoping it doesn't come with a 'mute' button!

- ❖ I've decided to open a lubricant shop outside government offices—there's a huge demand for greasing palms.

- When my kids were little, every room in the house was a Drawing Room.

- During rush hour, my breakfast consists of bread and traffic jam.

- Renaissance - the age in history when people began spelling difficult words.

- When it comes to un-dressing, there's nothing quite like a comic strip.

- My kids call our home 'motherland'—I guess they know where the real power lies!

- Stone Age - the modern times when police in battle gear face a violent mob armed with rocky missiles.

❖ The law of life: the pen by the phone never works, and if it does, the notepad's gone missing.

❖ My wife finds me irresistible… when she's not wearing her prescription lenses.

❖ Given the main activity, management suggests renaming the Meeting Room to the Eating Room.

❖ A cop pulled me over and asked, 'How are you?' I said, 'Fine!'—and so did he, for not wearing my seatbelt.

❖ Our fencing team is ready for the Olympics—they're already shopping for barbed wire!

❖ The religious sermon blaring through the loudspeakers? Pure 'sound' philosophy.

❖ Birthday: the day everyone celebrates you getting older.

❖ You're in grave danger if you stand too close while lowering the coffin.

❖ Cough formula: explaining $E=mc^2$ while battling a bad cold.

❖ Sky scraper - the guy who grates vegetables on the 95th floor.

❖ High jumpers might just stay above the poverty line, while pole-vaulters will never go hungry!

- ❖ The HR department isn't just hiring; it's also a fire station!

- ❖ Our tug-of-war celebration ended with the real winner: the guy who rented us the rope for a hefty fee!

- ❖ Banks report a stinky locker room—customers stuffed their lockers with onions as prices soared!

- ❖ Air conditioners cool you down, but the power bill will make you sweat!

- ❖ Strainer: someone who trains others with a whole lot of effort!

- ❖ An overcrowded bus-shelter? That's a full stop!

❖ With angry crowds confronting tainted ministers, rotten eggs are now pricier than regular ones!

❖ My two-footed wife was no match for the eight-footed baby spider—she screamed and ran for cover!

❖ I reserved two seats for my friend, rumoured to have a split personality!

❖ With my naturally expressionless wooden face, I was instantly chosen to sit at the government office reception!

❖ At a function, my wife mentioned her bad headache, and my friend asked if it was me!

- ❖ I asked the taxi driver for a place with good food, cheap deals, and a view without opening the door—he dropped me off at the Central Prison!

- ❖ While practicing Yoga, I got into the Lotus posture—and now I'm on leave because I can't untangle myself!

- ❖ I applied for the Environmentalist's award—I'm green with envy!

- ❖ Respect all religions—they bless you with holidays!

- ❖ Horror movies should charge half price—most viewers watch with their eyes half closed!

❖ I felt the irony when asked to calculate the 'carpet area' for 'below the poverty line' housing!

❖ Green tea: just glorified hot water!

❖ The Postal Dept. has a novel idea to boost sagging revenues: send anonymous letters urging folks to mail 25 copies to friends—fail to do so, and await the worst!

❖ To combat rising burglaries, I installed surveillance cameras—three days later, they were gone!

❖ At the meeting, the MC kept shouting, 'Give them a big hand!'—now I'm home hands-free!

- ❖ Minutes are the records of meetings that usually take hours or days to emerge!

- ❖ Can 'Kalashnikov' be found in an English dictionary? Sure—if it's big enough!

- ❖ Claiming I could solve the murder in no time, I turned to the ultimate detective, Google, and asked, 'Who committed the crime?'

- ❖ For the best in thrills, crime, suspense, comedy, and sex, tune into News Hour on any channel!

- ❖ ATMs: cozy air-conditioned cubicles for security guards to stretch out and snore—oh, and you can also withdraw money!

- ❖ Boring speakers in meetings? Perfect time to catch up on all your emails!

- ❖ In management class, they taught us to 'stay focused'—so I changed my lenses.

- ❖ Apart from being environmentally friendly, I've become quite rich thanks to my collection of money plants.

- ❖ Feeling hungry, I munched on a few chips off the old block.

- ❖ Avoid wearing bell-bottoms when you're trying to steal; they'll trip you up and give you away while you're running!

- ❖ The noble gases always lived in castles in the air, staying unreactive while others were busy bonding.

- ❖ In the noisy gym, I found peace among the dumbbells.

❖

- ❖ After waiting too long for my order at the restaurant, I ended up turning into a waiter!

- ❖ Slipper: someone who glides on banana peels!

- ❖ Stamp collector - The guy who fell down first and took the whole brunt of footfalls during a stampede.

- ❖ Driving school tip they missed: if you're in the wrong, just glare at the other driver like they've committed the worst crime!

- ❖ In the mosquito family tree, humans are now listed as blood relations!

- ❖ The glass being half full or half empty isn't the issue - it's what to fill the other half with!

- ❖ Swiss Blank - the amount of information one can get about the huge deposits in the financial houses tucked away in the Alps.

- ❖ To call me average is quite a mean thing to say!

- ❖ Procrastination: the word you'll spell… later!

- ❖ The Taj Mahal must be exhausted after posing for millions of photos over the years!

- ❖ Postman: the key player on the football team whose goal is to keep deliveries out of his post—also known as the goalkeeper!

- ❖ At five and a half feet long, I applied for a job as a measuring scale!

❖ Before marriage, I thought flying saucers came from outer space, piloted by aliens. After marriage, I realised they originate from the kitchen, operated by my wife during our fights.

❖ Handles are just layovers for bacteria hopping from hand to hand!

❖ Iron Man has a staple diet.

❖ MISSNG - Happened while I went for a walk.

❖ Reunited with an old college mate, we joyfully exchanged memories—and visiting cards—both eager to remember each other's names!

❖ Credit card: 'Neighbour's envy, owner's pain!'

❖ With this relentless rain lashing the city, we need to decide: build the Metro or the Ark?

❖ He-Man: the guy who's had his gender doubly checked!

❖ Priceless: The expression one displays at the checkout counter, finding that the Master credit card limit has exceeded.

❖ Curiosity killed the cat. Murder solved.

❖ Can moving from one failure to another in the shortest period be considered a success?

❖ For the highly stressed - it's past tense, present tense, and future tense.

❖ With all the stupid serials on TV, we could really use an ultimate serial killer!

❖ I really hate a speaker when the guy next to me falls asleep on my shoulder and starts to snore!

❖ I read it takes 62 muscles to frown and 26 to smile, so at the gym, I get my heavy workout frowning and a light one smiling while others just sweat!

- ❖ People who barely open their mouths must be calling their mother 'Mum.

- ❖ We're hosting a workshop on 'How to Get Rid of Superstition' tomorrow—just waiting for the astrologer to tell us the most auspicious time to start!

- ❖ Raavan Smiley :-):-):-):-):-):-):-):-):-)

- ❖ The meteorological department predicts heavy rain all week, so it's the perfect time to start painting the house!

- ❖ Our Olympic boxing team is ready—to pack up everyone else's medals and ship them out!

❖ To escape from prison, I managed to smuggle in a twelve-inch ruler, to scale the high walls.

❖ When onion prices soar, they bring tears to your eyes from miles away!

❖ The Public Works Dept.: where the public works to fill the potholes that crater the city roads during monsoon!

❖ I jumped into what I thought was my car, cranked the ignition, and was met by a scream—turns out I'd picked the wrong ride and the wrong wife.

❖ My wife and I went vegetarian for a month, and I overheard our dachshund Socrates saying to his friend, 'I smell a recession!'

❖ Earthquake: Nature's way of bringing man back down to earth!

❖ Seeing "Press Here" I pressed, suddenly a group of journalists appeared from nowhere and sat down around me.

❖ As the inches grow, the waist turns to waste!

❖ Belly dancers graduate from the Navel Academy.

❖ Bankers: the most 'interest'ing folks around!

❖ Who says plain is simple? I've spent a week piecing together a 550-piece puzzle of an empty blackboard!

❖ When I claimed politicians are the least corrupt, my lie detector short-circuited!

❖ Ever feel like you're the only sane driver on the road? Don't worry, we all feel that way!

❖ Thinking simply seems too complicated to practise.

❖ As I patted my bald head, I saw my wife swoon over a guy with luscious locks. 'Nice wig, right?' I whispered, dripping with envy.

❖ The judge had the final word—and it was a sentence!

❖ As a numismatist, I asked the tour guide for top coin collectors—he took me straight to the beggar colony!

❖ Just imagine Gandhari in the Mahabharatha trying to wake up and send 101 kids to school—now that's a morning nightmare!

❖ At a company function, when the mic tester shouted 'Check, check, check,' a swarm of vendors rushed to the stage—payment time!

❖ With just one child to marry off, the matrimonial ad could proudly say 'Limited Edition!'

❖ A narcissist is someone who posts on Facebook and then hits the Like button themselves.

❖ Home is where items with limited shelf life are stored for the rest of your life.

❖ With Heaven above and Hell below, is it any wonder we're stuck here with so many middlemen?

❖ Dysentery stood by the gate, keeping watch for his replacement, eager to rush off and relieve himself.

❖ Chronic horror movie viewers don't need nail clippers.

❖ Unlike other jobs, successful copywriters get their start in childhood, honing their skills by copying during class exams.

❖ Sometimes, I log into my wife's Facebook account and hit 'Like' on all my boring posts.

❖ After diving into online games, I ended up owning a whole city, a massive farm, and a fabulous roller-coaster theme park—too bad I lost my job while building my empire!

❖ My wife grants me the freedom to say anything—does that make me a free man or just a brave one?

❖ Mother tongue? Naturally!

- A shoe seller's dream: millipedes in stylish footwear!

- I've issued an ultimatum to my dog, cat, spiders, cockroaches, mice, mosquitoes, ants, and all other housemates: either chip in for the housing loan and taxes, or pack your bags!

- Newborns these days must think life is all about screens—Dad's on the laptop, Mom's on the mobile, grandparents are glued to the TV, and big brother's conquering the PlayStation!

- When I was young, I was encouraged to remember everything and store it in my mind. Now that I'm older, I'm told to forget the past and clear out the clutter!

❖ The zebra crossing must be a Christian

❖ I think we're practicing death by hanging instead of electrocution—thanks to the constant power interruptions in our area!

❖ Having a pair of hands and ten fingers has its perks—like covering my face and peeking through my fingers during horror movies!

❖ My wife claims she has 364 other days under her control—besides International Women's Day.

❖ The luckiest guys who get to pore over shapely figures at work? Accountants!

- Ego should have been spelled Igo!

- With so many fraudsters crawling the net, we should gift them unique IDs like gettricked.con or loseallyourwealth@africamail.con

- Call a spade a spade and experience the echo.

- To err is human; to err terribly is advanced technology.

- The doctor told me I have a stone in my kidney. Not bad—now I possess a secret weapon!

❖ I'm green with envy, blind with rage, and black and blue from yesterday's fight. Does that make me a physically challenged colourful personality?

❖ Are board meetings just misspelt?

❖ Inside the bars, mosquitoes fly zig-zag after biting the drunk patrons!

❖ My wife allows me to claim I'm the boss of the house.

❖ I wrote an autobiography, but when I checked its popularity at the public library, they directed me to the Comics section.

❖ He oohed and aahed over the shapely figures displayed before him—a true mathematician fanatic!

❖ When the wise speak, the wiser listen. But when the wiser talk, the wisest simply goes to sleep, with little else to do.

❖ I lied to my prospective employer, claiming I was absolutely honest. He said I was selected but never sent me the appointment letter!

❖ I received the most abridged version of the Mahabharata: a single piece of paper that read, 'An Indian family feud.'

- I can't believe I'm being arrested for starting my company, Sleeper Cells – I just wanted to offer travellers budget friendly naps.

- The cannibals wrapped up their dinner competition—it was a nail-biting finish!

- Running out of ideas, I think I'm ready for a marathon!

- I took a long rope and skipped dinner—talk about a real jump in my diet!

- Yesterday was Women's Day, but to my wife, the whole year is!

❖ I started a mental asylum exclusively for those who go bonkers managing too many WhatsApp groups!

❖ After hearing that too many cooks spoil the broth, I decided only my father would be employed in our family!

❖ You can't judge a book by its cover, but you can sure book a judge without cover.

❖ All the worms you see are the late risers—it pays to be lazy.

❖ I met a Swiss watchmaker in the middle of a desert. He specialized in making precise hourglasses.

❖ As a wedding photographer, I've witnessed a lot of matches.

❖ I saw the shark stifle a smile when someone on the ship cried out in panic, 'Man overboard!'

❖ I realized the kleptomaniac in me wasn't dead when, after my trip to the U.S., I found the Statue of Liberty in my garden.

❖ During the hot summer, every day feels like Fryday.

❖ I discovered an eco-friendly cure for jealousy—it makes you go all green with envy!

❖ From the way banks loot us, it seems they're hiring a few bank robbers too.

❖ The woodcutter who accidentally hit his head with an axe became a true split personality.

❖ When I arrived at the hospital 'Casualty' ward, I found all the patients were married.

❖ The bakery business? It's no cakewalk!

❖ Even as a strict vegetarian, I get butterflies in my stomach when it's time to speak!

❖ When skydiving, I'm truly a down-to-earth guy!

❖ Sitting in the back seat, I enjoy driving others mad.

❖ Against all odds, I decided to remain even.

❖ Constantly jumping to conclusions, I'm a qualified contender for the World Trampoline Championships!

❖ The biggest punctuation mark I know is the 100-meter dash.

❖ Once upon a time, I used to write novels, but the recession forced me into one-liners.

❖ My neighbour's data-friendly dog gave me a few bytes!

❖ I fenced my yard using the local latitudes and longitudes.

❖ I glared at him, told him his days were numbered, and gifted him a desk calendar.

❖ Thank God I'm an atheist!

❖ I fenced my yard using the local latitudes and longitudes!

❖ All the resumes I see are too perfect—it's like I've stumbled into a Utopian job fair!

❖ Two negatives is actually a positive sign – there's always hope.

- ❖ What's the height of luxury? It all depends on how high those letters are!

- ❖ I'm near certain that mosquitoes, flies, cockroaches, spiders, rats, and snakes bribed their way onto the Ark!

- ❖ When I'm doing nothing, I'm still doing something, right?

- ❖ I piled all my educational qualifications on top of common sense and buried it deep – hardly needed these days.

- ❖ With WA, FB, and other instant media, email feels as old-fashioned as a postcard!

- Learning to drive construction piles into the ground? Now that's a real bore!

- Rajnikanth can kill two birds with absolutely no stone!

- The last time I stopped asking my mother to do my homework was when she asked me to do hers instead!

- The Decathlon champion is truly a Jack of all trades.

- In the middle of the desert, I'm just waiting for the shipment to arrive.

- After extensive training and coaching, I finally joined the Railways.

- Now I'm just on the job of finding one!

❖ As a successful procrastinator, I always have something to look forward to doing tomorrow!

❖ I really hope the pizza delivery boy becomes a cop—he's already a pro at getting to places fast!

❖ They say too many cooks spoil the broth -- I allowed only my father to work in our family.

❖ Cornered by a lion, I hit the escape key on my laptop, and got away.

❖ To lose weight, I repeatedly watched The Battle of the Bulge.

❖ I still wonder why 'abbreviation' is such a long word?

- ❖ I know Karate and Judo—both Japanese, huh!?

- ❖ Didn't like what I saw in the mirror, so I changed the mirror.

- ❖ Ran into a prayer group... or so I thought. Turns out they were a smart phone congregation.

- ❖ All the worms you see? Just lucky late risers.

- ❖ A family- tree? The original theory of relativity.

- ❖ The astrologer said a whole new world was coming for me. How did he know I was getting new glasses?

- I became a quiz master because... I had no idea what the answers were.

- Invented an air-tight container, but somehow the news leaked.

- Where there's a will, there's a way... and a long queue of relatives.

- I prayed to be invisible. Now I'm a ghost—be careful what you wish for!

- Settled on the couch with pizza, wafers, and Coke—ready for the grueling task of watching the Olympics.

- Just thinking about walking a hundred miles was enough to exhaust me.

❖ Humpty Dumpty's problem? He was treated by horses and soldiers instead of doctors.

❖ When my grandson wouldn't stop crying, I pulled out my secret weapon—my Aadhaar card photo. Laughter guaranteed!

❖ In traffic jams, I follow my cardiac surgeon friend—he's an expert in bypasses.

❖ I'm so lazy I placed an ad in the paper... for a nail cutter, with a nail cutter.

❖ I think cats are terrified of vacuum cleaners. Mine vanishes as soon as I point the nozzle.

❖ I store all my secrets in a folder labelled 'Instruction Manual.' No one's ever opened it.

❖ I plan to serve humanity after death… as a skeleton key.

❖ I bowed in respect to the pizza that fed a family of four.

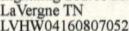

www.ingramcontent.com/pod-product-compliance
Lightning Source LLC
LaVergne TN
LVHW041608070526
838199LV00052B/3037